First U.S. edition 2020
First published by Nosy Crow Ltd. (U.K.) 2020

Library of Congress Catalog Card Number pending
ISBN 978-1-5362-1219-8

19 20 21 22 23 24 25 APS 10 9 8 7 6 5 4 3 2 1

Printed in Humen, Dongguan, China

This book was typeset in Filson Pro.
The illustrations were created digitally.

Nosy Crow
an imprint of
Candlewick Press
99 Dover Street
Somerville, Massachusetts 02144

www.nosycrow.com
www.candlewick.com

Natalie Labarre, who made this book, is an
ILLUSTRATOR and **ANIMATOR**. These two jobs
mean she gets to draw and tell stories all day for
advertising, films, and books. Natalie is obsessed with
unusual jobs because she was so relieved when she
finally found out that you can draw for a living!

INCREDIBLE JOBS YOU'VE (PROBABLY) NEVER HEARD OF

BY: natalie labarre (me)

nosy crow

An imprint of Candlewick Press

The GREAT

doctor   lawyer   farmer

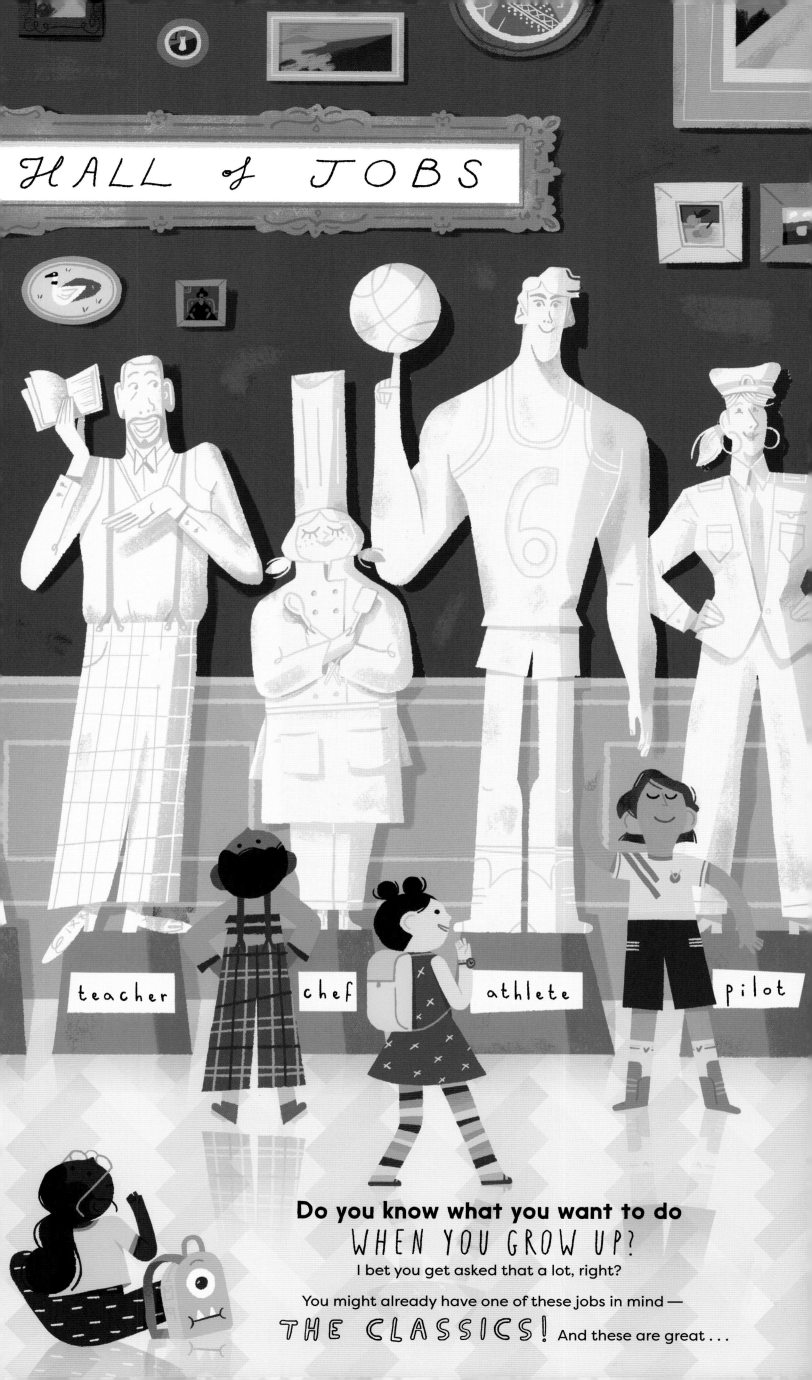

But did you know that there are ALL SORTS of incredible jobs out there that you've probably never heard of?

One of them might be just right for you!

HIGH-RISE WINDOW WASHERS need more than a ladder to reach these windows. They work suspended in midair as high as 1,000 feet (300 meters) up — except when it's too windy!

For the most expensive beef in the world, **COW MASSAGERS** in Japan make sure their cows are as relaxed as possible by giving them regular massages.

Can you spot people doing these jobs?
Find them again later in the book
to learn more about them.

- Line Sitter
- Garbage Detective
- Body Farmer
- Golf Ball Diver
- Ski Patroller
- Sloth Nanny
- Water Slide Tester
- Bicycle Fisher
- Nautical Cowboy
- Smoke Jumper

FUNERAL CLOWNS are paid to lighten the mood on difficult days. Wearing bright clothes and playing tricks, they help people to remember their loved ones with a smile.

MUSEUM

Using a feather duster, this **DINOSAUR DUSTER** keeps the dinosaur bones in the natural history museum spotless. They're 145 million years old, so he has to be extremely careful. No shaky hands!

Believe it or not, Queen Elizabeth II owns all of the swans in the U.K.! Every year, a **WARDEN OF THE SWANS** catches each one living near Windsor Castle, checks their health, marks them, and sets them free. This ceremony is called Swan Upping.

There are **11 swans** in this scene. Can you find them all?

TOPIARY ARTISTS have been around for thousands of years. They use special tools to sculpt bushes into fancy shapes, and their work can be found in places from castle gardens to Disneyland!

Jobs can come in ALL SHAPES AND SIZES—it just depends on what you're looking for!

What about something . . .

CREATIVE?

A **WIG MAKER** sews thousands of real human hairs into a very fine mesh that is the shape of the soon-to-be wearer's head. Then the wig is styled just the way the client likes it. The new hairdos can sit on the heads of anyone from stage actors to cancer patients.

METICULOUS?

At some lakes during spawning season (when fish lay their eggs), you can catch a **FISH COUNTER** carefully keeping track of life underwater. Wildlife experts record the numbers of different species to help keep their populations from being affected by overfishing.

MYSTERIOUS?

CRYPTOZOOLOGISTS try to find evidence of creatures from myths and legends that others don't think are real, like Bigfoot or the Loch Ness Monster. Actual zoologists call their work pseudoscience since it can't be proven by scientific fact — but don't tell them that!

Coconuts for horse hooves, flapping gloves for bird's wings — these are just some of the tricks a **FOLEY ARTIST** might use to record sound effects for Hollywood films. The method is named after famous sound effect artist Jack Foley, who worked on movies in the 1920s.

DANGEROUS?

If found, even a 100-year-old bomb, land mine, or grenade left over from a long-ago war could explode at any time. An **UNEXPLODED ORDNANCE TECHNICIAN** specializes in safely investigating and removing any dangerous unexploded devices. Phew!

OR FABULOUS?

Can you spot the difference between a quickly fading fad and a trend that's here to stay? Leave it to a **TREND SPOTTER** to always know what's cool and what's not. This information can be worth billions to the most cutting-edge brands.

With some jobs . . .

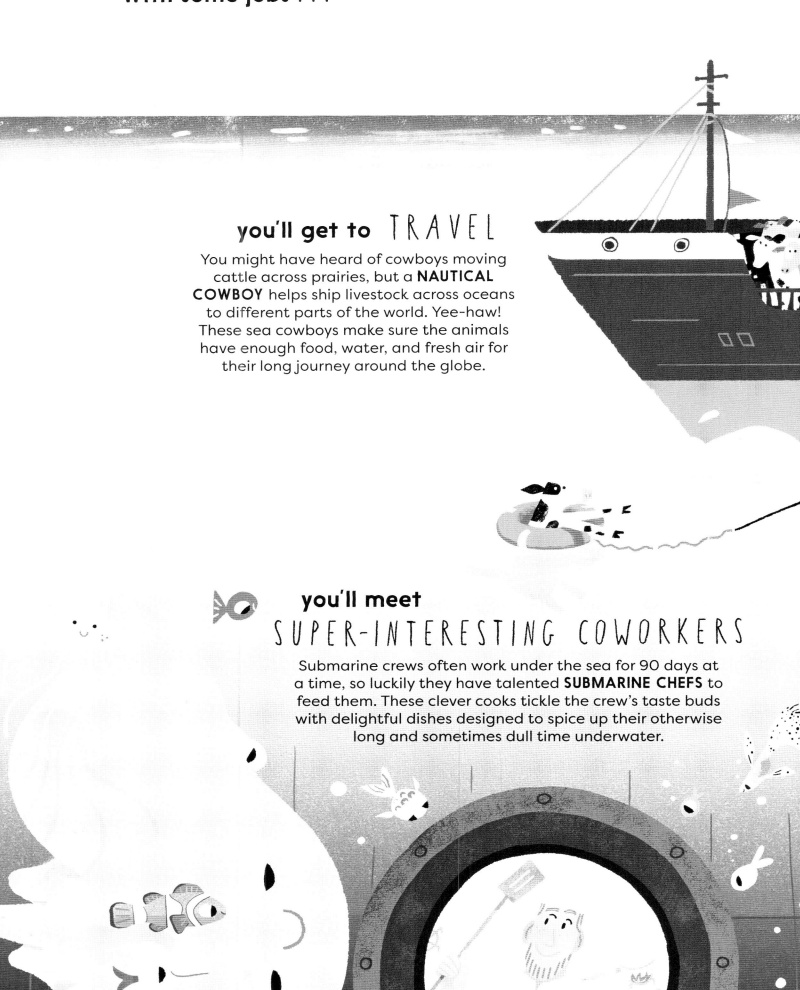

you'll get to TRAVEL

You might have heard of cowboys moving cattle across prairies, but a **NAUTICAL COWBOY** helps ship livestock across oceans to different parts of the world. Yee-haw! These sea cowboys make sure the animals have enough food, water, and fresh air for their long journey around the globe.

you'll meet

SUPER-INTERESTING COWORKERS

Submarine crews often work under the sea for 90 days at a time, so luckily they have talented **SUBMARINE CHEFS** to feed them. These clever cooks tickle the crew's taste buds with delightful dishes designed to spice up their otherwise long and sometimes dull time underwater.

you'll learn NEW SKILLS

Have you ever heard of milking a snake? **SNAKE MILKERS** spend years training to carefully collect deadly venom from poisonous snakes by having them bite down on a covered glass jar! The poison can be used for many things, such as medical research and making antivenom to treat snakebites. A patient suffering from a snakebite might last as little as two hours if they're not treated in time, so get milking!

Some jobs happen
high above...

Mount Rushmore, in South Dakota, is a huge stone sculpture of four past American presidents, and **CRACK FILLERS** work to stop the historic landmark from crumbling. The repair team uses silicone sealant to fill cracks in the stone as high up as 5,700 feet (1,700 meters). Even enormous stone faces need a little facial now and again!

You don't look a day over two hundred, Mr. President!

while others operate
w a y   u n d e r g r o u n d.

In Tokyo, Japan, the trains are so crowded during morning and evening rush hours that white-gloved **TRAIN PUSHERS**, or *oshiya*, actually push people on board. The *oshiya* pack the trains tight and make sure nobody gets caught in the doors. It's a tight squeeze for people hoping to get to work on time, as the trains are filled well beyond their capacity!

Some underground jobs are more GRUESOME than others.

If you get scared stiff at the thought of working with dead bodies, then being a **BODY FARMER** might not be for you. When people donate their bodies to scientific research, they might end up in a body farm. Here, scientists recreate crime scenes, study how bodies decompose, and collect data helpful to criminal investigations.

You're just in time — let me give you the tour!

Plenty of people wish they could live forever. If they have enough money, they could hire a **CRYONICS TECHNICIAN** to freeze their head shortly after they've died. The heads are kept at a steady –328°F (–200°C) in the hope that one day technology will be advanced enough to bring their preserved brains back to life.

27   28   29   30

Who better to ask about the wonders of preservation than an **EGYPTOLOGIST**? These experts study all aspects of ancient Egypt, including mummification. In 1994, a leading Egyptologist mummified a real human in the ancient Egyptian way — the first person to do so in 2,000 years. YIKES!

Most people can't bear the thought of living without their furry loved ones — and they don't necessarily have to. When the time comes, a **PET PRESERVATIONIST** could turn a poodle into a taxidermy masterpiece by stuffing its body or even freeze-drying it!

Too grisly? Fair enough. How about some quirky jobs for the TALENTED WRITERS among you?

A lot of thought goes into being a **NAIL POLISH NAMER**, which is actually often a group effort. The team behind a new nail color comes up with ideas together, even taking trips to find inspiration for the perfect name. It's got to be catchy, because memorable names can boost sales by a lot!

Fire-Cracker Red

MORE PE
PLEAS

HOORAY! YOU'RE OLDER NOW!

GREETINGS! — HERE'S A CARD!

A feeling is an idea with roots.

According to **FORTUNE COOKIE WRITERS**, a good fortune has got to be thought-provoking, a little surprising, but also vague AND relatable to whoever ends up opening it. Not easy! But someone has to come up with the messages for the 3 billion cookies made each year!

Laura from down the hall doesn't actually like your new shirt.

Eat your vegetables — or else!

Ghoul Gray

MONKEY SNACKS

SNOW DAY

≥ YOU'RE ≤

GRAPE !!

What better way to show your true feelings to a loved one than by having a complete stranger write something for you? A **GREETING CARD WRITER** comes up with clever or thoughtful messages so you don't have to. Thank goodness! Full-time writers can produce two to twenty cards per week!

A **CROSSWORD PUZZLE WRITER** can spend anywhere from a week to a month making the perfect puzzle for cruciverbalists (otherwise known as people who love solving crosswords) to figure out — go figure!

Does all that writing sound like hard work?
How about doing a job that DOESN'T SOUND LIKE A JOB at all?

Some jobs sound like fun and games. A **TOY DESIGNER** needs a big imagination to come up with toys that everybody wants. They also need good mechanical skills and an expert knowledge of how children play.

The job of a **TOY BREAKER** is to take all of that hard work and smash it to bits! It may be messy, but it's important for making playtime safe. Toys are tested to see how long they last, and reports are written about any potential dangers.

Imagine if it was your job to live in paradise! **ISLAND CARETAKERS** look after incredible places to keep them in tip-top shape. Some islands are super luxurious, while others are a little wilder and call for outdoorsy skills. Either way, you can't beat ending the workday with a sunset on the beach.

The most-fun-job award probably goes to **WATER SLIDE TESTERS**. Water parks and travel companies actually pay people to test some of the craziest slides around the world. Testers check for safety, speed, and creative features, and there's a scale to rate the "splash factor" and "adrenaline levels."

The Nose Dive

Rapunzel's Escape

The Medusa

Looking for even more of A THRILL?

When a forest fire occurs in a remote area, specialized firefighters called **SMOKE JUMPERS** parachute in from planes or helicopters to fight the blaze. Working in small groups and wearing extremely heavy equipment, smoke jumpers can spend days putting out the fire!

Or maybe you'd rather CHILL?

PROFESSIONAL SLEEPERS get paid to snooze — for scientific research, to test new sleep medicine, or even to report on new sleep products. It might sound dreamy, but it's not always! In 2017, NASA ran a study that would help to keep astronauts safe in space: they paid 12 volunteers to stay in a bed tilted upside down for 30 days straight!

Are you a particularly P A T I E N T person?

Oh, perfect! Have you ever thought of becoming a **TORTOISE WALKER**? In New York City, the owner of a tortoise named Henry hires someone to walk him in the park. According to his owner, the walker has to be good with animals and with people, too, because everyone likes to stop and chat with their unusual reptilian neighbor.

If you're patient and you also happen to love cleaning, an **IMAX SCREEN CLEANER** position could be a great fit. It takes about eight hours to clean dust, food, and even spit off the 72 x 53 foot (22 x 16 meter) screen. That's as tall as a five-story building!

Are you that person who sings Christmas songs all year round? Do you have a different ugly Christmas sweater for every day of the week? Well, you're going to love this! At a big supermarket in Wales, you can get a job as a **CHRISTMAS LIGHT UNTANGLER** if you can untangle 10 feet (3 meters) of lights in under three minutes!

As a **LINE SITTER**, you could get paid to stand in line to buy the latest gadget or food craze for someone else. It could take minutes or even hours. By the time you get to the front of the line, you should be able to afford as many "conuts" as you want!

Third time in this line today. I'm going to be rich!

What about joining the Golden Gate Bridge's painting squad? In San Francisco, a team of **BRIDGE PAINTERS** continuously repaints the iconic landmark. With 600,000 rivets in one tower alone, it's no small task, but the glorious view probably makes up for it.

Perhaps you are more of a $VISUAL$ person?
What about a job with a little
MORE COLOR?

Over time, paintings can fade or become damaged or dirty. **PAINTING RESTORERS** are trained to bring an artwork's colors back to life without changing or harming the original. They tailor their approach to each piece based on the materials and methods used to create it. A word of caution: leave it to the professionals! In Spain in 2012, an elderly parishioner tried to restore a fresco of Jesus that was over 100 years old. Instead she made him look like an alien monkey!

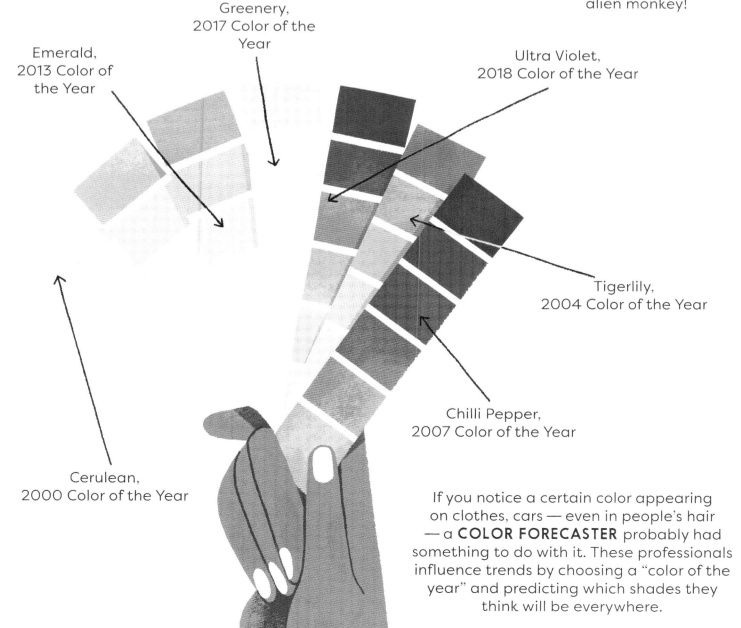

Greenery,
2017 Color of the Year

Emerald,
2013 Color of the Year

Ultra Violet,
2018 Color of the Year

Tigerlily,
2004 Color of the Year

Cerulean,
2000 Color of the Year

Chilli Pepper,
2007 Color of the Year

If you notice a certain color appearing on clothes, cars — even in people's hair — a **COLOR FORECASTER** probably had something to do with it. These professionals influence trends by choosing a "color of the year" and predicting which shades they think will be everywhere.

Every color has a distinct personality and can affect the way we feel. That's why some people hire a **COLOR CONSULTANT** when redecorating. These experts get to know their clients and the mood they want to create, then choose a color scheme that makes them feel at home.

Maybe ANIMALS are more your thing?

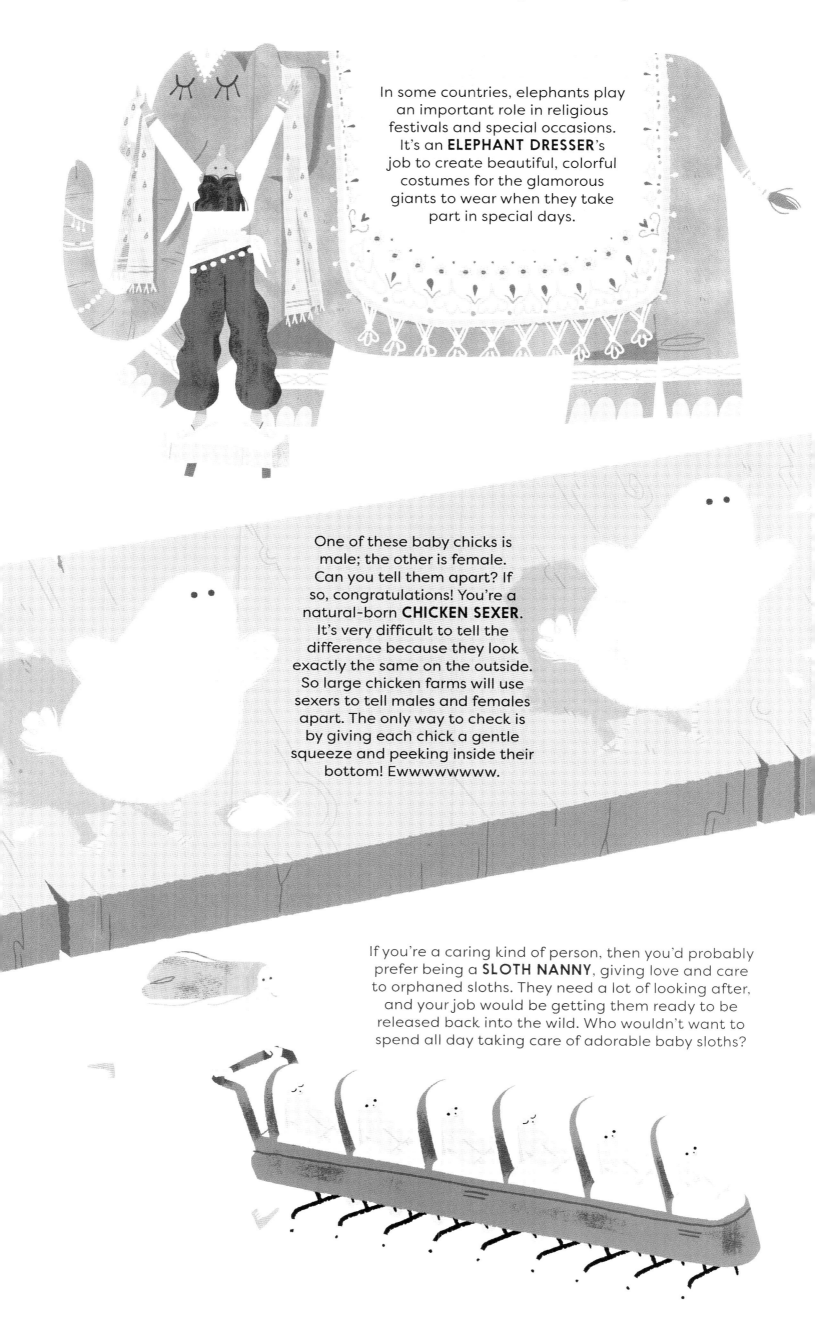

In some countries, elephants play an important role in religious festivals and special occasions. It's an **ELEPHANT DRESSER**'s job to create beautiful, colorful costumes for the glamorous giants to wear when they take part in special days.

One of these baby chicks is male; the other is female. Can you tell them apart? If so, congratulations! You're a natural-born **CHICKEN SEXER**. It's very difficult to tell the difference because they look exactly the same on the outside. So large chicken farms will use sexers to tell males and females apart. The only way to check is by giving each chick a gentle squeeze and peeking inside their bottom! Ewwwwwwww.

If you're a caring kind of person, then you'd probably prefer being a **SLOTH NANNY**, giving love and care to orphaned sloths. They need a lot of looking after, and your job would be getting them ready to be released back into the wild. Who wouldn't want to spend all day taking care of adorable baby sloths?

-Heidi-
The cross-eyed opossum

LASSIE

DOLLY

-Mr. Ed-

PIZZA RAT

Eddie

Thelma and Elise

LONESOME -George-

CHOUPETTE

SONYA The slow loris

SINGING JACK

BABE

Bubbles

Are you always staring at other people's pets? Well, that creepiness could turn into a career! An **ANIMAL TALENT AGENT** searches for cute animals that belong in front of a camera. An agent can provide trained animals of all types — from dogs and cats to more exotic species — for film, television, photo shoots, theater, and more.

Can you guess what a **BIOLOGICAL RESOURCE SPECIALIST** does? Give up? That's the official title for an airport scarecrow — a real person whose job it is to make sure birds don't get in the way of landing or departing planes, for both animal and human safety. When birds are on the runway, the scarecrow rushes to the scene and makes a lot of noise to frighten them away. Shoo!

Some jobs are
OUT OF THIS WORLD!

Being cramped in space for long periods of time is no easy ride. That's why astronauts rely on a **SPACE PSYCHOLOGIST** to keep track of their mental health before, during, and after every space mission. While in space, there are many home comforts that an astronaut might miss (like toilets and showers), but a space psychologist will talk them through any stress or emotional strains.

A **SPACE SUIT ENGINEER** gets the crew looking their best just in case we make contact with another planet. It's important to make a good first impression! Just kidding! The designer mostly focuses on how the suit will work as a piece of equipment for life in space, but it still looks pretty awesome, too.

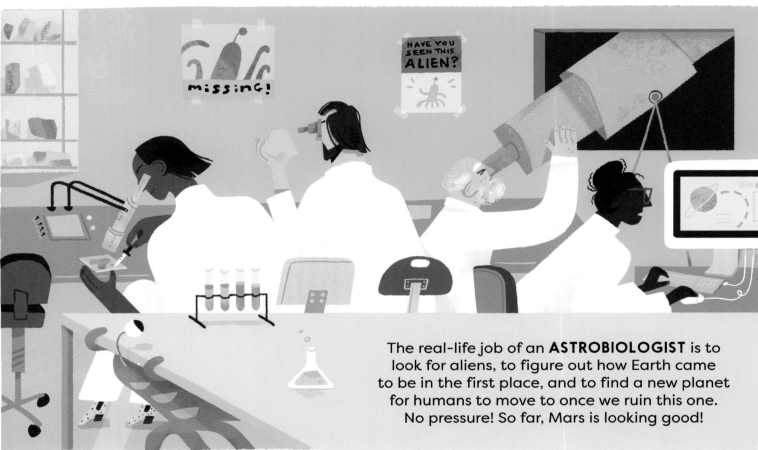

The real-life job of an **ASTROBIOLOGIST** is to look for aliens, to figure out how Earth came to be in the first place, and to find a new planet for humans to move to once we ruin this one. No pressure! So far, Mars is looking good!

Once a spacecraft is launched, any smells inside it get stronger and stronger. That's because it's such a small space and it's very hot — a bit like when you're in a car for a long time. Since it wouldn't be a bright idea to roll down a window, NASA uses a **CHIEF SNIFFER** whose job it is to smell-check anything that'll be on the ship. He's taken part in more than 850 smell missions since 1974!

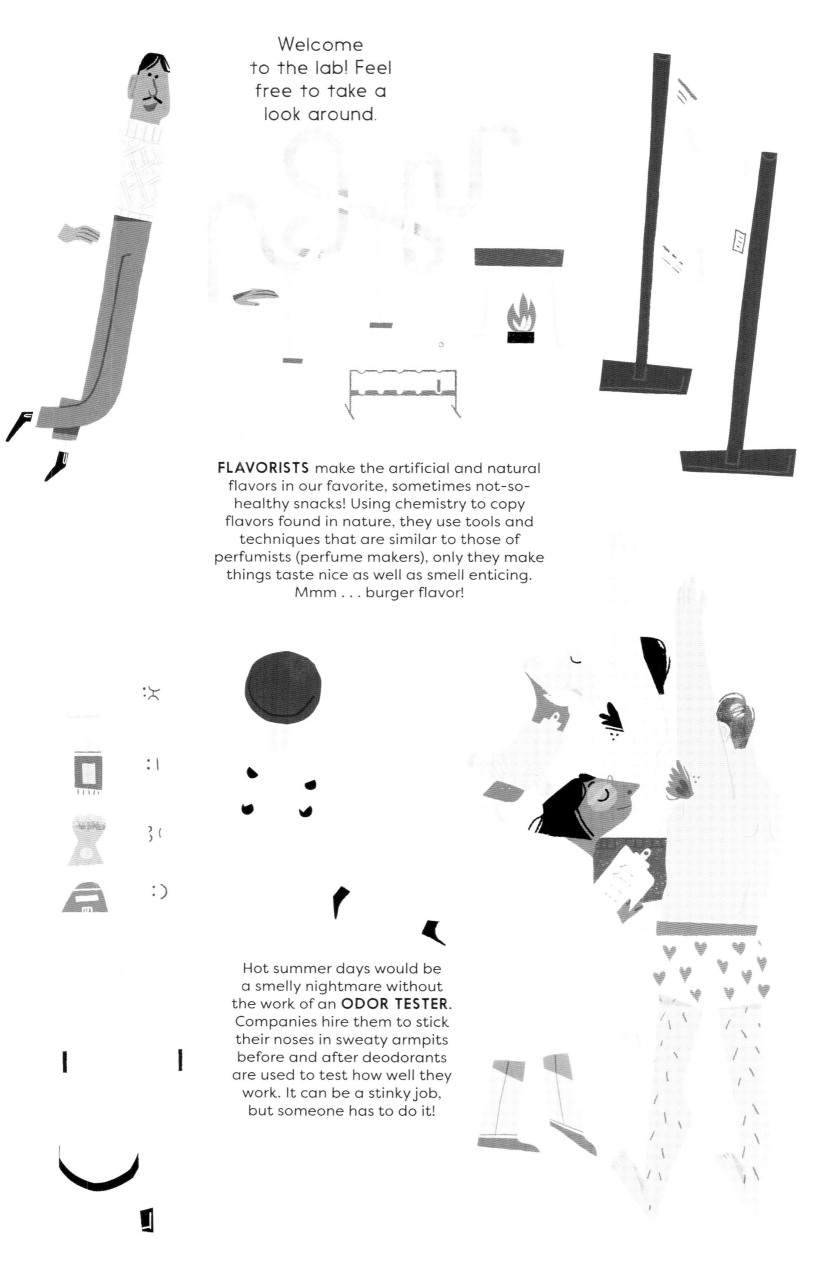

Welcome
to the lab! Feel
free to take a
look around.

FLAVORISTS make the artificial and natural flavors in our favorite, sometimes not-so-healthy snacks! Using chemistry to copy flavors found in nature, they use tools and techniques that are similar to those of perfumists (perfume makers), only they make things taste nice as well as smell enticing.
Mmm . . . burger flavor!

Hot summer days would be a smelly nightmare without the work of an **ODOR TESTER**. Companies hire them to stick their noses in sweaty armpits before and after deodorants are used to test how well they work. It can be a stinky job, but someone has to do it!

Now you might think this looks a bit odd, but this **FACE FEELER** is actually hard at work. Also known as sensory scientists, they touch people's faces to test how well different skin-care products work — everything from face cleansers and moisturizers to razors and peels.

Picky eaters beware! **TASTE TESTERS** analyze products with their expert tongues, from medical studies where you might get paid to eat only fast food for three months, to testing food that's not even real food, like dog food! Tasting requires a lot of concentration, and they need to take good care of their 10,000 taste buds, resting between courses and avoiding anything too spicy or salty.

Another scientifically smelly job is that of a **BREATH ODOR EVALUATOR**, who takes a whiff of somebody's breath before and after they have used a product, like chewing gum or mouthwash. Their job is to figure out the difference and rate the smell each time.

Whether you're in a
SMELLY LAB or
BUSY WORKSHOP,
the right setting is key
to a job well done!

Can you match these
five people to their
WORK SPACES?

"Can you think of anything more beautiful than making something old as good as new again? Neither can I — as a matter of fact, I transform things for a living! Artists and writers send me their tools, and I freshen them up and send them back, always with shavings as a 'certificate of sharpening.'"

A

"Oh, don't mind me . . . I'm not breaking the law. I'm just breaking into a system. But don't worry: it's my job! Companies pay me to check for problems or weak spots and then fix them before any real thieves give it a try."

B

"EYE can see you! I just love that joke, but being hilarious is not all I do! I start by taking measurements, and then I make a model and paint it as realistically as possible. SEE what I mean?"

C

"I can stomach the most squeamish of snacks! My hard work goes into those disgusting moments on TV that might make you look away. I am hired to try things out — several times — just to make sure they're safe for celebrity challenges."

D

"If you see someone in trouble on the slopes, you'd better give me a call! In an emergency, I rescue people who have gone missing on the mountain and can provide first aid. Sometimes I even get to trigger avalanches so nobody else does accidentally. It's pretty COOL!"

E

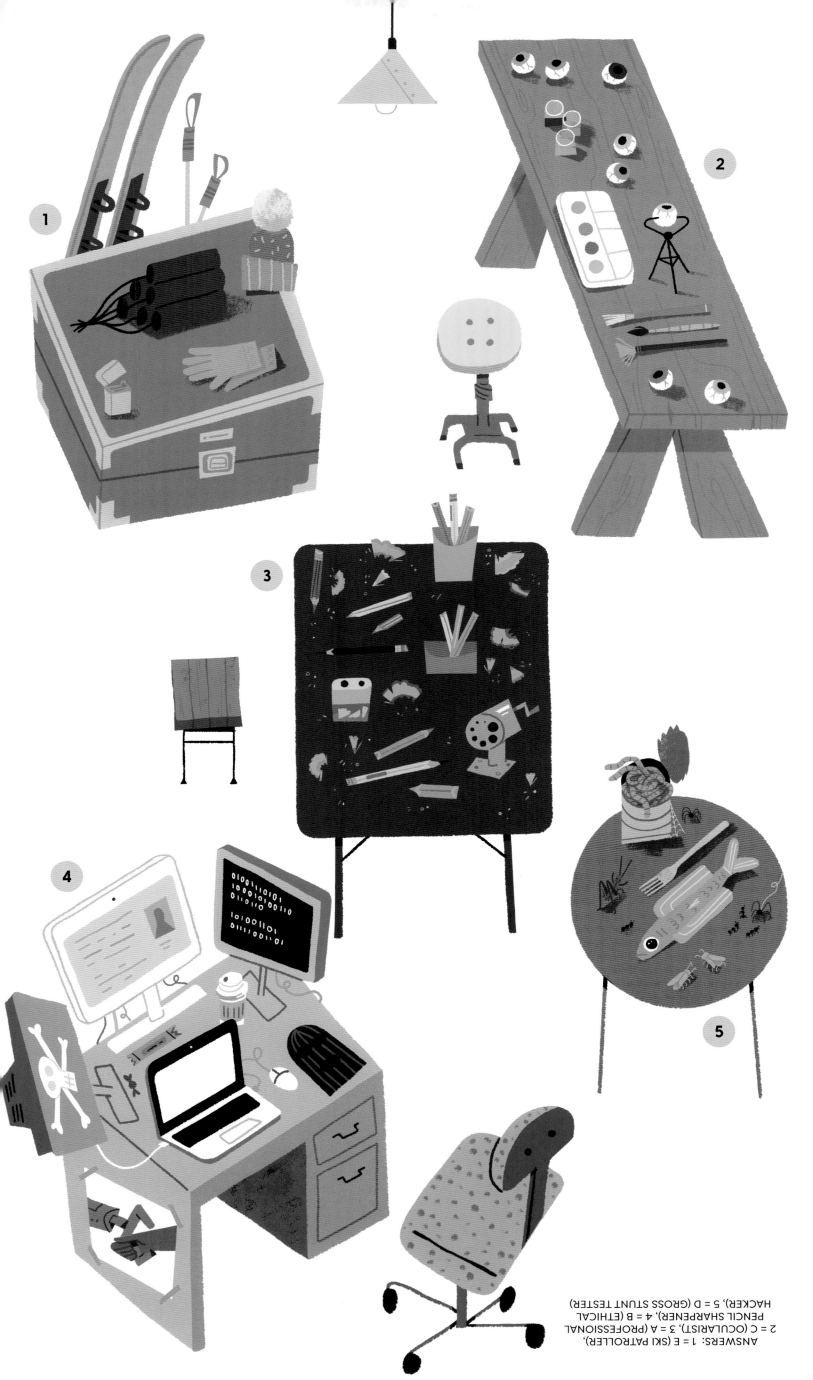

Some workplaces are W E T T E R than others. It's amazing what you can find when you're F I S H I N G for it.

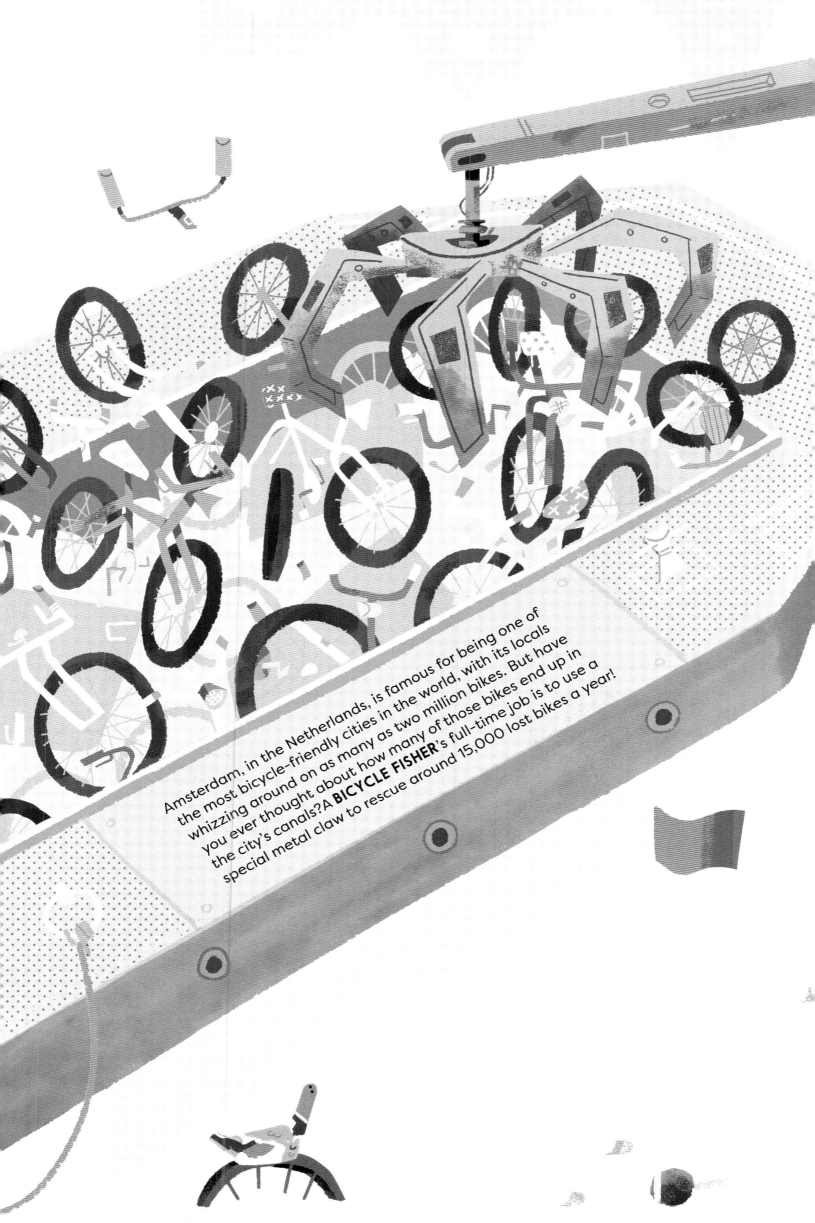

Amsterdam, in the Netherlands, is famous for being one of the most bicycle-friendly cities in the world, with its locals whizzing around on as many as two million bikes. But have you ever thought about how many of those bikes end up in the city's canals? A **BICYCLE FISHER**'s full-time job is to use a special metal claw to rescue around 15,000 lost bikes a year!

I like to think that bikes make for much better wishes than coins.

Here's a completely different type of fishing: **GOLF BALL DIVERS** pay a fee to golf courses so that they are allowed to spend eight to ten hours a day plundering their ponds. That's because these professional recyclers can make a lot of money cleaning, packaging, and reselling any golf balls they find lurking in the deep water. Just watch out for alligators!

This diver has dropped **6 golf balls** on the other pages of this book. Can you find them?

If you don't mind fishing through other people's garbage, you could be someone who ENFORCES THE RULES...

In Germany, where you'll find some of the world's strictest recycling laws, **GARBAGE DETECTIVES** take their job very seriously. They're always on the lookout for things that aren't thrown away correctly. (Batteries in the trash? Outrageous!) They dig through bins, check shopping receipts, and even question nosy neighbors to find evidence of trash-can crimes!

or maybe you'd rather be someone who BREAKS THEM!

This guy gets paid to jump on the bed! But he's not monkeying around. **MATTRESS JUMPERS** use their feet to check for any lumps in the filling. They have to be able to feel even a pea-size lump! They're careful and precise with their jumps, using a grid pattern so they don't miss a spot.

Meanwhile, this woman plays with her food — professionally! To help sell cheese, supermarkets sometimes hire a live **CHEESE SCULPTOR** to create amazing works of art from cheese. The carved sculptures can also be used at special events, like food festivals. It's Brie-lliant!

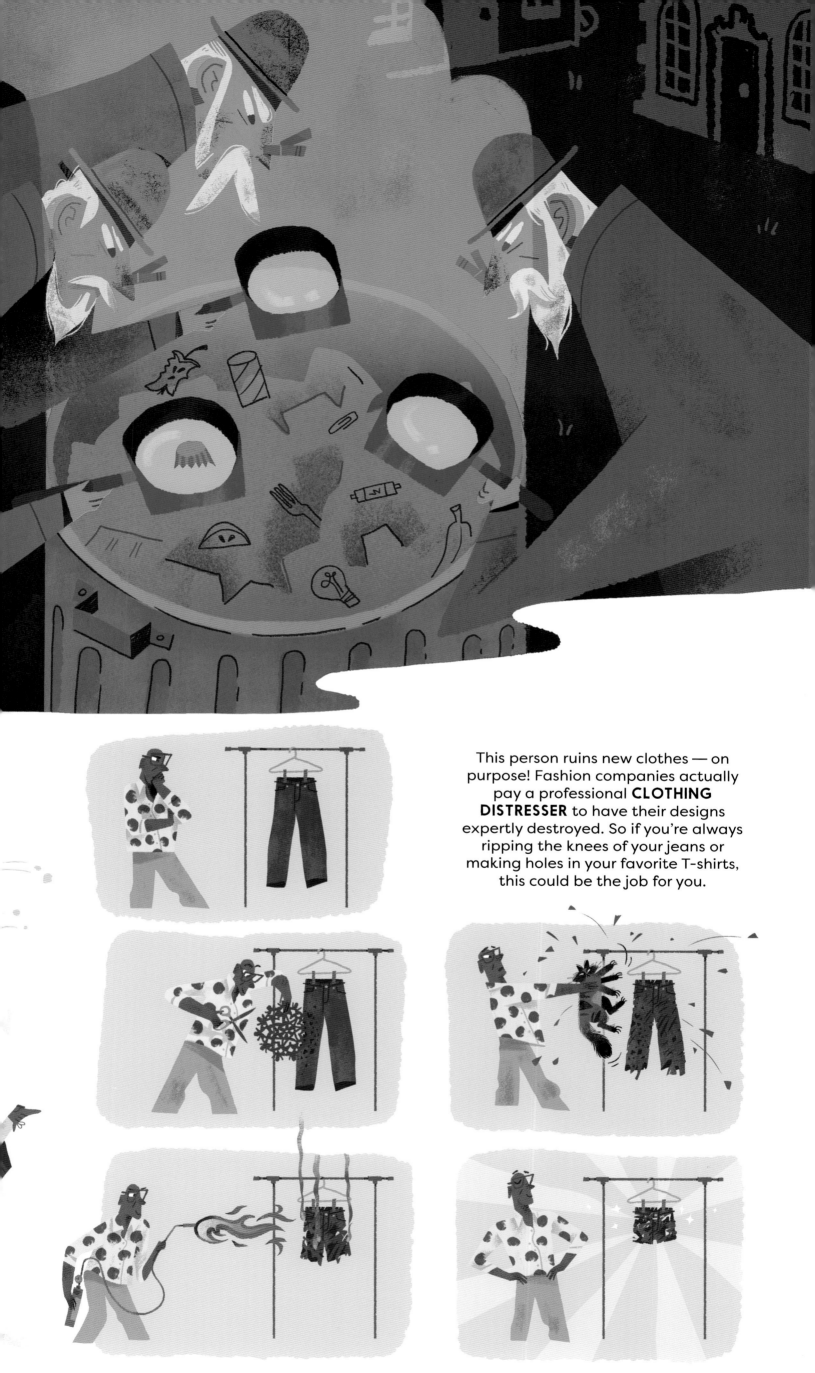

This person ruins new clothes — on purpose! Fashion companies actually pay a professional **CLOTHING DISTRESSER** to have their designs expertly destroyed. So if you're always ripping the knees of your jeans or making holes in your favorite T-shirts, this could be the job for you.

Hands off THESE CLOTHES!
These people can't do their jobs without them!

Can you guess what they do based on their UNIFORMS?

1

2

3

"I wouldn't be able to do my job without my suit. I need to wear it so that artists can use the tracking points to animate crazy features on top of my movements. At least that's what they told me — it could also just be a prank!"

A

"Some say only fools rush in to get married by the king of rock 'n' roll, Elvis Presley, but I say it's now or never! Viva Las Vegas!"

B

"My job dates back almost 200 years. What do I do? I wake up Queen Elizabeth II every morning at 9 a.m. I stand under her window for about 15 minutes. Works every time."

C

ANSWERS: 1 = F (POLICE DOG HANDLER), 2 = E (SWISS GUARD), 3 = A (MOTION CAPTURE ACTOR), 4 = B (LAS VEGAS WEDDING MINISTER), 5 = C (PIPER TO THE SOVEREIGN), 6 = D (SKY WAITER)

4

5

6

"I've got a head for heights, which is lucky because I wait on tables that are suspended by a crane 164 feet (50 meters) in the air. Guests are strapped into the flying dinner table like a roller coaster as I serve them a three-course meal!"

D

"My role is to protect the pope himself. Dating back to 1506, we're one of the oldest military units in the world. You won't find an army today with a heavier or more complicated uniform: it's made from over 150 pieces and weighs as much as four bags of sugar!"

E

"It takes weeks to train a new police dog so they can use their incredible sense of smell to help us search for things. I wear this uniform to protect myself when 'bite sleeve training'— that's when we teach the dog to growl and attack if we're in danger."

F

Jobs aren't always easy — and sometimes they can even be QUITE EMOTIONAL!

It's usually not a great idea to cry at work, unless you're a **PROFESSIONAL MOURNER**, that is. Also called moirologists, these people are hired by the family of someone who has died if they're worried that not many people will turn up at the funeral. Their job is to cry for Aunt Betsy and pretend that they were friends or family. The mourner is even armed with a fake story in case any real friends and family become suspicious.

Aunt Betsy
Kids x 2
Golfer
Hated cyclists

Putting together a wedding can be stressful. It's no wonder some brides would prefer to trust a **PROFESSIONAL BRIDESMAID** to help with the preparations rather than their lovely but unqualified friends. These pros can step in if the maid of honor starts panicking, and they can help with things like speech writing, dress shipping, or even keeping the peace in the bridal party before the big day.

It can be tough to say you're sorry, but if you find it easy, you could become a **PROFESSIONAL APOLOGIZER**. You could work as a customer service employee for a large company like an airline, or in Japan, there are even special apology agencies that can get people to say sorry on your behalf — for anything!

Laughter is contagious. That's why television shows with a live studio audience hire **PROFESSIONAL LAUGHERS** to get everybody going! They can burst out hearty and infectious laughter on command. It's not as easy as it sounds: Can you try laughing as loud as you can right this second?

JOBS

hef ... thlet ... pilot ... plumber ... ba
da

Oh, look!
Here comes
a fresh
one!

vlogger

clown

skier

park ranger

mime artist

Don't worry if you still don't know what your DREAM JOB might be.

All the jobs in this book are as UNIQUE as the people who do them.

The trick to choosing the right job for you, no matter how unusual, is to know yourself.
What do you LOVE to do? Do you know what you're good at?
In a constantly changing world, there are brand-new jobs popping up ALL the time!

And of course, you can always change your mind if you want to give something
else a try later on down the line. There are NO RULES!
You don't have to stick with one job forever. Give many things a try to see what you like best!

**And if the job you want doesn't even exist yet,
you could be the one to make it happen!**